50 THINGS YOU SHOULD KNOW ABOUT AMERICAN PRESIDENTS

by Tracey Kelly

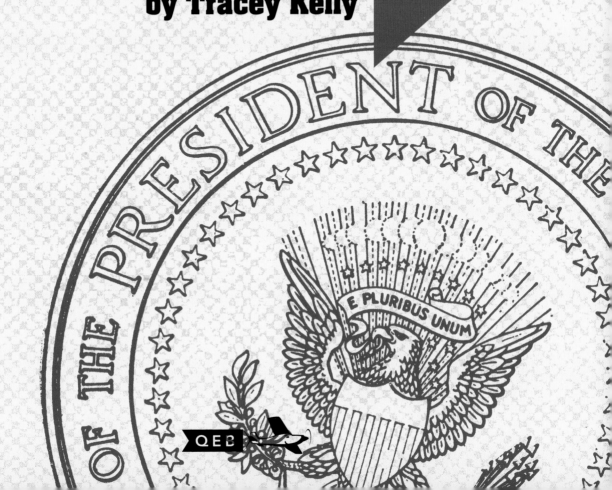

PRESIDENT OF THE

OF THE

E PLURIBUS UNUM

QEB

Publisher: Maxime Boucknooghe
Editorial Director: Victoria Garrard
Art Director: Miranda Snow
Project Editor: Sophie Hallam
Design and Editorial: Tall Tree Ltd
Consultant: Dr. Timothy C. Hemmis

Published in the United States by
QEB Publishing, Inc.
6 Orchard Road
Lake Forest, CA 92630

A CIP record for this book is available
from the Library of Congress.

ISBN 978 1 60992 936 7

Printed in China

Words in **bold** are explained
in the glossary on page 78.

CONTENTS

The U.S. Government

The United States of America uses a system of government called **representative democracy**, with its principles set out in a document called the **Constitution**. There are three branches of government—legislative, executive, and judicial. They all work together in a system of checks and balances to ensure power is shared equally and fairly.

EXECUTIVE BRANCH

The President of the United States heads the executive branch, aided by the Vice President and the **Cabinet** members, who are in charge of different departments. The Cabinet advises the President and helps carry out decisions. Independent agencies also help with decision-making and perform special services.

▼ *The White House is the official residence of the U.S. President.*

LEGISLATIVE BRANCH

The legislative branch of the United States government makes the laws. Its key body is **Congress,** which has two parts: the House of Representatives and the Senate. Voters elect two senators for each state and several state representatives based on each state's population. Only Congress can declare war.

▲ *Congress sits in the U.S. Capitol in Washington, D.C.*

There are many political parties in the United States, but the Democratic and the Republican parties are the main two. Each **party** has a different viewpoint on issues that affect laws and shape people's everyday lives. U.S. citizens are free to join any party they like.

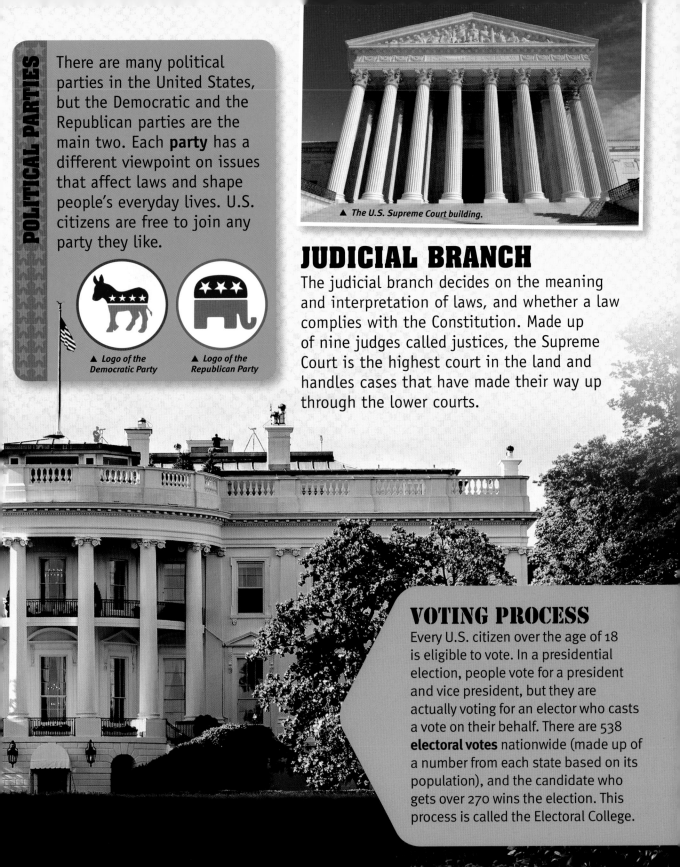

▲ Logo of the Democratic Party

▲ Logo of the Republican Party

▲ The U.S. Supreme Court building.

JUDICIAL BRANCH

The judicial branch decides on the meaning and interpretation of laws, and whether a law complies with the Constitution. Made up of nine judges called justices, the Supreme Court is the highest court in the land and handles cases that have made their way up through the lower courts.

VOTING PROCESS

Every U.S. citizen over the age of 18 is eligible to vote. In a presidential election, people vote for a president and vice president, but they are actually voting for an elector who casts a vote on their behalf. There are 538 **electoral votes** nationwide (made up of a number from each state based on its population), and the candidate who gets over 270 wins the election. This process is called the Electoral College.

A New Nation

①

MASSACHUSETTS (MAINE)

NEW YORK (VERMONT)

NEW HAMPSHIRE

▼ Map showing the original 13 colonies that formed the new nation of the United States of America.

MASSACHUSETTS

NEW YORK

RHODE ISLAND

CONNECTICUT

NEW JERSEY

DELAWARE

MARYLAND

PENNSYLVANIA

VIRGINIA

NORTH CAROLINA

SOUTH CAROLINA

GEORGIA

KEY

Original 13 colonies

Non-settled territory

| 0 | | | 300 miles |
| 0 | | | 500 kilometers |

The first colonists from Europe reached the Americas during the 1500s, taking land from Native American peoples. By the mid-18th century Britain was the dominant colonial power in North America, but its subjects were becoming resentful of British rule.

◀ British "redcoat" troops surrender in 1781 after the Battle of Yorktown, the last major battle of the Revolutionary War.

FREEDOM

In 1763, after winning a costly war against France, Britain raised taxes unfairly on its American colonies. This angered the colonists. In 1773, a group of Bostonians threw a cargo of highly taxed tea into Boston Harbor. Britain's response was brutal. In 1775, the 13 colonies united to fight the Revolutionary War, which established the United States as a new independent country.

KEY EVENTS

★ **APRIL 19, 1775**
The Revolutionary War begins (see page 8).

★ **JULY 4, 1776**
The Declaration of Independence is signed (see page 7).

★ **APRIL 30, 1789**
George Washington becomes first U.S. President (see page 8).

★ **SEPTEMBER 25, 1791**
The Bill of Rights is introduced (see page 7).

GOVERNMENT

The colonists made their key break with the British crown on July 4, 1776, when they signed the **Declaration of Independence**. Among those who signed were two future presidents—John Adams and Thomas Jefferson. Another decisive document was the Constitution of 1787—which forms the basis of law in the United States. It was followed by a **Bill of Rights** in 1791, a set of amendments to the Constitution that protected people's rights. However, the new nation was divided over the issue of **slavery**, which was used in the plantations of the Southern states.

BANISHED

Native Americans found that they could not stay neutral in the American Revolution. The Six Nations Confederacy of Native American peoples—the Seneca, Cayuga, Onondaga, Oneida, Mohawk, and Tuscarora—were the strongest Native American group in the northeast of America. When the colonists started fighting each other, they initially tried to stay neutral. But they were soon forced to take sides in battle. No provisions were made for them when the war ended, and those who had backed the British had to give up their land.

▲ *Thayendanegea, also called Joseph Brant, was a Mohawk leader who fought on the British side.*

▼ *George Washington, the United States' first President (standing on the right), oversees the signing of the U.S. Constitution at Independence Hall, Philadelphia, in 1787.*

JULY 4, 1803
The Louisiana Purchase (see page 13).

JUNE 18, 1812
The War of 1812 begins (see page 14).

MARCH 3, 1820
Congress passes the Missouri Compromise (see page 15).

MAY 28, 1830
The Indian Removal Act is signed, beginning the Trail of Tears (see page 17).

George Washington 1789–1797

George Washington

Born into a wealthy planter family in Virginia, George Washington was one of the Founding Fathers of the nation. His strong leadership carried the **Continental Army** to victory in the Revolutionary War in 1781. He helped draft the Constitution and served two terms as the United States' first president.

▼ *On the night of December 25–26, 1776, Washington led his troops across the Delaware River to carry out a surprise attack on British forces and their allies.*

COMMANDER

As a landowner at Mount Vernon, Washington felt that British imperial regulations were unfair. He became a key figure in the uprising against Great Britain in the 1770s. He was elected Commander in Chief of the Continental Army in 1775 during the American Revolution. In 1781, he led the American army to victory against the British at Yorktown, Virginia.

Washington introduced the cabinet system, as well as the title "Mr. President."

CONSTITUTION

In 1787, Washington led the Constitutional Convention in Philadelphia. At this important meeting, the delegates agreed to draft a new Constitution— the document on which the laws and principles of the United States are based, even to this day.

RELUCTANT LEADER

When the Revolutionary War ended, Washington wanted to return to his wife, retire from public life, and farm his plantation at Mount Vernon. But he soon realized that the new nation needed his leadership and experience. By a unanimous vote, Washington was elected to lead the country. At his **inauguration** on April 30, 1789, standing on the balcony of the Federal Hall on Wall Street, New York, he swore the oath to become first President of the United States.

▲ *Washington arrives for the first inauguration.*

FAST FACTS

1st President of the USA
Born: February 22, 1732
Died: December 14, 1799
Terms (two): 1789–1797 **Party:** None
First Lady: Martha Dandridge Custis
Vice President: John Adams

PARTY SPLIT

By the end of President Washington's first term in office, two parties with differing political ideologies began to emerge. Washington was dismayed—he felt this would disrupt the unity of the nation.

▼ *Alexander Hamilton (left) and Thomas Jefferson, the leaders of the USA's first rival political parties.*

John Adams
1797–1801

Born in Quincy, Massachusetts, John Adams was highly intelligent and went to Harvard at age 15, later studying law. He was a passionate patriot and a delegate at the **Continental Congress** between 1774 and 1777. Afterward, Adams was a diplomat in Europe, then first Vice President under George Washington.

▶ The house where John Adams was born, now part of the Adams National Historical Park.

FAST FACTS
2nd President of the USA
Born: October 30, 1735
Died: July 4, 1826
Term: 1797–1801 **Party:** Federalist
First Lady: Abigail Smith
Vice President: Thomas Jefferson

UNPOPULAR LAW
In 1798, President Adams approved laws that meant the U.S. government could imprison or send home "dangerous" foreign immigrants. The Alien and Sedition Acts were unpopular and helped Adams lose his reelectio[n] campaign to Thomas Jefferson, his own Vice President!

▼ The U.S.S. Constitution was one of six warships built for the new U.S. Navy in the 1790s.

FRENCH CONFLICT

After the Revolutionary War, the U.S. Navy was disbanded. However, by the time John Adams became President, there was a new war raging between France and Britain, and American ships were often attacked by pirates. In order to deter the pirates, and to strengthen the nation's defenses in case it was drawn into a conflict, Adams founded the Department of the Navy. He also ordered the construction of six new ships, including the warship U.S.S. *Constitution*. As a result, Adams is sometimes referred to as the "Father of the American Navy."

GREAT WRITER

After his presidency, John Adams retired with Mrs. Adams to Quincy and spent the next 25 years writing books, columns, and letters to his old friend and rival Thomas Jefferson. Fifty years after the Declaration of Independence—on July 4, 1826— Adams died, saying, "Thomas Jefferson survives." But he did not realize that Jefferson had died earlier that day.

NEW HOUSE

When President Adams moved into the new White House on November 1, 1800, it was damp and half-finished—the city of Washington was also under construction. He wrote to his wife, Abigail Adams, "May none but honest and wise Men ever rule under this roof."

Thomas Jefferson 1801–1809

When he became President in 1801, Thomas Jefferson had already served as Governor of Virginia, Secretary of State, and Vice President—not to mention the author of the Declaration of Independence. His presidency saw the USA grow vastly in size following the Louisiana Purchase.

Thomas Jefferson

FAST FACTS

3rd President of the USA
Born: April 13, 1743
Died: July 4, 1826
Terms (two): 1801–1809
Party: Democratic-Republican
First Lady: Martha Wayles Skelton
Vice Presidents: Aaron Burr 1801–1805, George Clinton 1805–1809

▲ Monticello, the house designed by Jefferson, is now a tourist attraction.

Because he was a powerful writer, Thomas Jefferson was chosen to be the main author of the Declaration of Independence. The document made it clear that the United States was a separate country from Great Britain and that it no longer had to follow British laws. It was signed on July 4, 1776, which is still celebrated today in the USA as Independence Day.

CHURCH AND STATE

As governor of Virginia for two years, Jefferson helped set up the "separation between church and state," so that people were free to choose their religion. He also campaigned for free public education—a radical idea at the time.

LAND PURCHASE

In 1803, President Jefferson had the opportunity to expand the USA westward when he agreed to buy the Louisiana Territory from Napoleon, the French Emperor. This huge area stretched across the middle of the country, covering part or all of 15 present-day states. The USA paid less than 3 cents an acre for the land—about $15 million ($240 million today)! Jefferson commissioned two men, Meriwether Lewis and William Clark, to explore the new territory. During their two-year journey, they met with at least 55 Native American tribes and learned about the land from them.

◄ *Acquiring Louisiana doubled the size of the United States of America.*

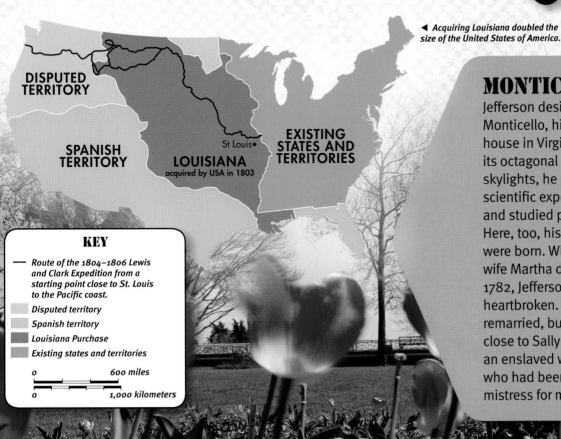

DISPUTED TERRITORY

SPANISH TERRITORY

St Louis•

LOUISIANA
acquired by USA in 1803

EXISTING STATES AND TERRITORIES

KEY

— Route of the 1804–1806 Lewis and Clark Expedition from a starting point close to St. Louis to the Pacific coast.

  Disputed territory

  Spanish territory

  Louisiana Purchase

  Existing states and territories

0   600 miles

0   1,000 kilometers

MONTICELLO

Jefferson designed Monticello, his unique house in Virginia. Amid its octagonal rooms and skylights, he performed scientific experiments and studied philosophy. Here, too, his children were born. When his wife Martha died in 1782, Jefferson was heartbroken. He never remarried, but remained close to Sally Hemings, an enslaved woman, who had been his secret mistress for many years.

James Madison
1809–1817

James Madison is best known for helping to draft the U.S. Constitution and for being the main author of its first ten amendments, known as the Bill of Rights. He is often called the "Father of the Constitution," despite his protest that it was "the work of many heads and many hands." An educated man with a degree from Princeton, he also served as Secretary of State under Jefferson.

◄ *Portrait of President Madison commissioned by his successor, James Monroe.*

WAR OF 1812
Great Britain was at war with France in 1812, and U.S. ships and cargoes were being seized along sea trade routes. So in June of 1812, President Madison declared war against Britain. British ships raided ports along the East Coast, also torching the White House in Washington. In 1814, the war ended with a peace treaty.

FAST FACTS
4th President of the USA
Born: March 16, 1751
Died: June 28, 1836
Terms (two): 1809–1817 **Party:** Democratic-Republican
First Lady: Dolley Payne Todd
Vice Presidents: George Clinton 1809–1812, Elbridge Gerry 1813–1814

HELLO, DOLLEY

Dolley Payne Madison was the first president's wife to be referred to officially by the title "First Lady." Her charm and political know-how did much to win allies for her husband. Intelligent and social, she hosted parties and even helped settle political quarrels. When the British burned the White House, Mrs. Madison bravely saved important documents.

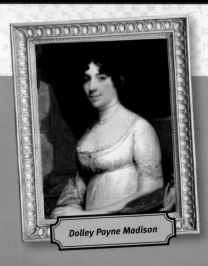

Dolley Payne Madison

James Monroe
1817–1825

James Monroe

Born in Virginia, James Monroe was an early revolutionary, fighting against the British while still a student. He became an officer in the Continental Army in 1776, serving alongside George Washington. Known for his honesty, Monroe worked as a diplomat, governor, senator, and cabinet official before becoming President in 1817.

FREE STATES

In President Monroe's term, five states joined the **Union**: Mississippi, Illinois, Alabama, Maine, and Missouri. Some were in favor of slavery, some were against it. The Missouri Compromise was a **bill** that allowed Missouri to become a slave state, but ensured that any new states north and west of Missouri became **free states**—slavery free.

FAST FACTS
5th President of the USA
Born: April 28, 1758
Died: July 4, 1831
Terms (two): 1817–1825 **Party:** Democratic-Republican
First Lady: Elizabeth Kortright
Vice President: Daniel D. Tompkins

DISPUTED TERRITORY

UNORGANIZED TERRITORY acquired by USA in Louisiana Purchase of 1803

MISSOURI

SPANISH TERRITORY

ARKANSAS TERRITORY

Missouri Compromise Line

◄ Map showing the extent of the USA in Monroe's time.

KEY

Existing states and territories closed to slavery
Existing states and territories open to slavery
Unorganized territory closed to slavery
Unorganized territory open to slavery
Disputed territory
Spanish territory
Missouri Compromise Line

0   600 miles
0   1,000 kilometers

NO TRESPASSING

EUROPE OUT

President Monroe passed an important foreign policy that barred European countries from claiming any more land in North and South America. Called the Monroe Doctrine, it prevented Spain from claiming more land in South America and Russia from taking land south of Alaska.

President Monroe pressured Spain into selling its Florida territories to the United States.

John Quincy Adams
1825–1829

As a child, John Quincy Adams experienced the presidency close up through his father, President John Adams. He traveled in Europe meeting leaders and royalty, and at just **26** years old, was appointed Minister to the Netherlands. Known as a fiercely independent diplomat, he served as Secretary of State and was elected President in **1825**.

John Quincy Adams

AMERICAN PLAN

As President, Adams felt it was important for the government to back programs that would improve American life. He proposed the building of new roads and canals, and national institutions for the arts and sciences. But because he had few political allies in Congress, many of President Adam's bills did not pass.

FAST FACTS

6th President of the USA
Born: July 11, 1767
Died: February 23, 1848
Term: 1825–1829
Party: Democratic-Republican
First Lady: Louisa Catherine Johnson
Vice President: John C. Calhoun

▼ *The Chesapeake & Ohio Canal is now a national park.*

C&O

President Adams opened the ceremony for the construction of the Chesapeake & Ohio (C&O) Canal on July 4, 1828. Funded by private and public money, this important trade waterway stretched for 185 miles.

CHARLES F. MERCER

Andrew Jackson
1829–1837

Brought up in the wild backwoods of the Carolinas, Andrew Jackson was the son of poor Irish immigrants and orphaned by the age of 14. He studied law and opened a successful practice in Tennessee. Known for his hot temper, Jackson notoriously killed a man in a duel over a horse race.

WAR HERO

During the War of 1812, Andrew Jackson was a major general in the U.S. Army, leading inexperienced volunteers in the fight against the British. Outnumbered two to one, Jackson and his men defeated the British at the Battle of New Orleans. He became a national hero overnight, which helped him win the presidency in 1829.

FAST FACTS
7th President of the USA
Born: March 15, 1767
Died: June 8, 1845
Terms (two): 1829–1837
Party: Democratic
First Lady: Rachel Donelson Robards
Vice Presidents: John C. Calhoun 1829–1832, Martin Van Buren 1833–1837

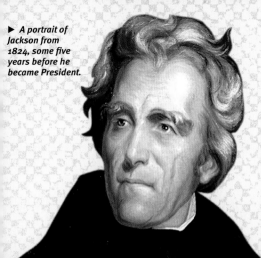

▶ A portrait of Jackson from 1824, some five years before he became President.

▲ Cherokee Native Americans are forced from their land in the 1830s.

TRAIL OF TEARS

On May 28, 1830, President Jackson signed the Indian Removal Act, which forced the Choctaw, Cherokee, Seminole, Chickasaw, and Creek to leave their lands within state borders and move to present-day Oklahoma. In 1838, around 4,000 Cherokee died of starvation and illness during their journey, which became known as the "Trail of Tears."

Martin Van Buren 1837–1841

Martin Van Buren

Martin Van Buren became leader of a political group called the "Albany Regency" that controlled New York politics in the 1820s. By 1829, he had become President Andrew Jackson's Secretary of State and in 1833, his Vice President. Van Buren was so respected that Jackson called him "a true man with no guile."

FAST FACTS

8th President of the USA
Born: December 5, 1782
Died: July 24, 1862
Term: 1837–1841
Party: Democratic
First Lady: Hannah Hoes
Vice President: Richard M. Johnson

ANTISLAVERY STANCE

President Van Buren was so strongly opposed to the expansion of slavery that he prevented Texas from being annexed (joined to the Union) because he was afraid it would become a slave state. He also worried that it would invite a war with bordering Mexico.

▶ *A cartoon shows Van Buren trying to bridge the gap between the proslavery and antislavery parties.*

William H. Harrison
March–April 1841

With aristocratic planter origins in Virginia, William Henry Harrison studied classics, history, and medicine. In his late teens, he suddenly decided to become a junior officer in the Regular Army and was stationed in the Northwest. There, he fought Native American tribes for land in the Ohio territories at the Battle of Fallen Timbers.

◄ Harrison's presidency lasted just 32 days.

FAST FACTS

9th President of the USA
Born: February 9, 1773
Died: April 4, 1841
Term: March–April 1841 **Party:** Whig
First Lady: Anna Tuthill Symmes
Vice President: John Tyler

SHAWNEE BATTLE

In 1801, Harrison became Governor of the Indiana Territories and tried to obtain more land from tribes so that people from the East could safely settle there. Shawnee chieftain Tecumseh formed a confederacy to try and stop the settlers. However, Harrison, as commander of the Army of the Northwest, defeated and killed Tecumseh at the Battle of the Thames in 1813.

SHORTEST PRESIDENCY

William Henry Harrison won the presidency by a huge majority. At 68 years old, he was the oldest man to be elected President. Sadly, he was also to serve the shortest time in office. On April 4, 1841, after just over a month in the White House, he became sick with pneumonia and died.

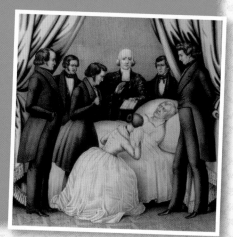

► Harrison's wife Anna weeps at his bedside as the President lies dying.

11

Westward Expansion and the Civil War

In the 1840s and 1850s, the United States expanded rapidly westward. Settlers started **homesteads** in the new frontiers, often coming into conflict with Native American tribes. By the mid-19th century, U.S. territories stretched from the Atlantic to the Pacific.

▼ *Map showing how the United States expanded westward during the first half of the 19th century.*

OREGON TERRITORY 1846 (Treaty with Great Britain)

NEW TERRITORIES

The USA expanded its territory both by cession (where a country signs a treaty to give up land) and annexations (where land is taken without a formal treaty). The 1846 Oregon Treaty settled an argument with Britain about the border between the USA and Canada. That same year, the USA fought a war with Mexico over land in California and New Mexico, eventually buying it from Mexico at a discount.

SPANISH CESSION 1819 ——

MEXICAN CESSION 1848

PURCHASE FROM MEXICO 1853

▲ *Slaves working the fields during the Civil War.*

THE NORTH-SOUTH DIVIDE

The addition of territories raised the question of whether slavery should be made illegal or allowed to continue in new states. Politicians tried to compromise, passing laws that let states decide for themselves. But this widened the gap between **abolitionists** in the North and proslavery supporters in the South.

KEY EVENTS

★ **1846**
The Oregon Treaty and war with Mexico (see page 23).

★ **SEPTEMBER 1850**
The Compromise of 1850 (see page 25).

★ **MAY 30, 1854**
The Kansas-Nebraska Act (see page 26).

★ **APRIL 12, 1861**
The Civil War begins with an attack on Fort Sumter (see page 28).

▲ Fought in Virginia, the Battle of the Wilderness in 1864 was one of the bloodiest battles of the Civil War.

CIVIL WAR AND AFTERMATH

Beginning in 1861, the war between the Confederacy of Southern states and the Union of Northern states devastated the country. In 1865, the Union won, leading to African Americans being freed from slavery and protected by the 13th, 14th, and 15th Amendments. The rebuilding of the South would take years, and the fight for African-American rights had only just begun.

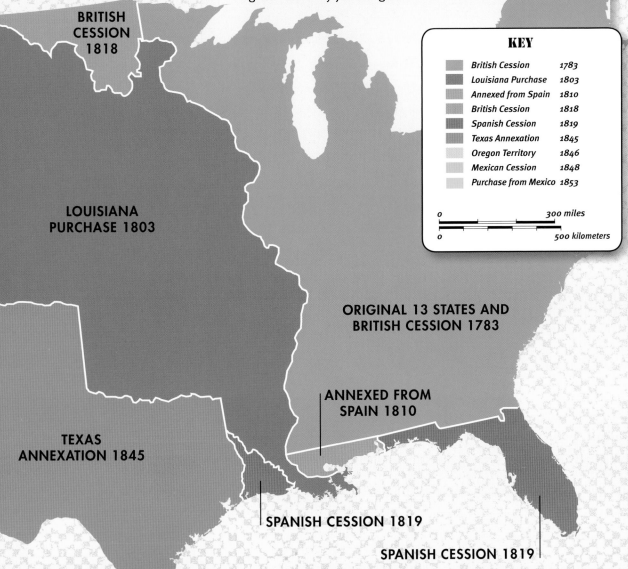

BRITISH CESSION 1818

LOUISIANA PURCHASE 1803

KEY

	British Cession	1783
	Louisiana Purchase	1803
	Annexed from Spain	1810
	British Cession	1818
	Spanish Cession	1819
	Texas Annexation	1845
	Oregon Territory	1846
	Mexican Cession	1848
	Purchase from Mexico	1853

0   300 miles
0   500 kilometers

ORIGINAL 13 STATES AND BRITISH CESSION 1783

ANNEXED FROM SPAIN 1810

TEXAS ANNEXATION 1845

SPANISH CESSION 1819

SPANISH CESSION 1819

JANUARY 1, 1863
The Emancipation Proclamation (see page 29).

JANUARY 31, 1865
The 13th Amendment abolishes slavery nationwide (see page 29).

APRIL 9, 1865
The South surrenders, ending the Civil War (see page 31).

FEBRUARY 3, 1870
The 15th Amendment gives African Americans the vote (see page 31).

21

John Tyler 1841–1845

Having served in the House of Representatives and later as Governor of Virginia, Tyler became the first Vice President to become President after the death of his predecessor. A keen expansionist, his most notable achievement was the annexation of Texas into the USA.

VETO POWER

President Tyler believed the Constitution should be strictly followed. He was a strong-willed leader who failed to approve many bills that Congress wanted to pass. After he vetoed the formation of a National Bank, the **Whigs** expelled him from their party, and most of his Cabinet resigned.

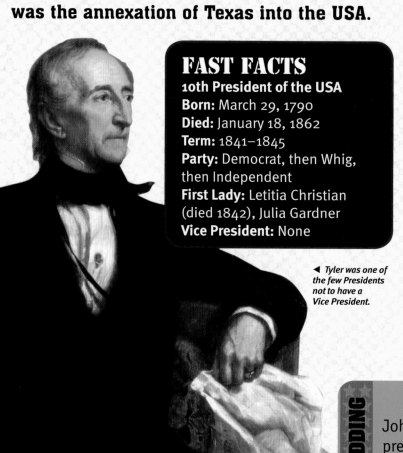

FAST FACTS

10th President of the USA
Born: March 29, 1790
Died: January 18, 1862
Term: 1841–1845
Party: Democrat, then Whig, then Independent
First Lady: Letitia Christian (died 1842), Julia Gardner
Vice President: None

◀ Tyler was one of the few Presidents not to have a Vice President.

Julia Gardner

SECRET WEDDING

John Tyler was the first president to marry while in office, after the death of his first wife, Letitia Christian. On June 26, 1844, he secretly wed the vivacious Julia Gardner, who was 30 years younger.

James K. Polk
1845–1849

From North Carolina, James K. Polk entered politics in the Tennessee legislature and served in the House of Representatives. When he ran for President, his friend Andrew Jackson backed him. The Polk presidency was marked by battles for new land.

◄ President Polk added a vast area to the USA.

FAST FACTS

11th President of the USA
Born: November 2, 1795
Died: June 15, 1849
Term: 1845–1849 **Party:** Democratic
First Lady: Sarah Childress
Vice President: George M. Dallas

LAND BATTLE

Polk wanted to expand America to the west and south, so in 1845 he sent an envoy to Mexico to offer $20 million for land in California and New Mexico. Mexico refused to sell and in 1846 its forces attacked U.S. troops as they entered disputed territory claimed by Mexico.

MORE STATES

President Polk's land expansion policy led to more tension between the North and South over whether slavery should be legal. He also risked war with Britain over acquiring the Oregon Territory, which stretched from the top of California to Alaska. But the Oregon Treaty in 1846 agreed the final border between the United States and Canada.

▼ U.S. troops (in blue) defeated the Mexican forces. Mexico was forced to sell New Mexico and California for $15 million.

First Lady Sarah Childress Polk helped write the President's speeches and gave him advice.

Zachary Taylor 1849–1850

▶ *Zachary Taylor dressed in his U.S. Army uniform.*

Zachary Taylor grew up in the wilds of Kentucky and later became a U.S. Army general. He spent 25 years guarding the frontier against attacks by Native Americans and fought in the Mexican War. In 1849, he was elected President largely because of his war hero record.

SECESSION THREAT

President Taylor was against slavery in new states joining the Union. He backed a law that would allow California to write its own constitution (and make slavery illegal). Anger was growing between Northern and Southern states, but Taylor made it clear he would use armed force to prevent states from leaving the Union.

FAST FACTS

12th President of the USA
Born: November 24, 1784
Died: July 9, 1850
Term: 1849–1850 **Party:** Whig
First Lady: Margaret Mackall Smith
Vice President: Millard Fillmore

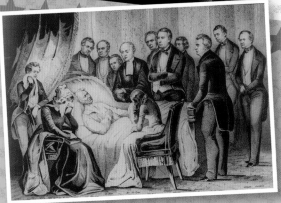

EARLY END

On July 4, 1850, Taylor's presidency came to an abrupt end when he got sick during a ceremony and died five days later. He had been strongly opposed to the South seceding from the Union, but 11 years later, his only son became a general in the **Confederate** army.

▲ *President Taylor on his deathbed, surrounded by his family and cabinet members.*

Millard Fillmore 1850–1853

Millard Fillmore

From humble beginnings in a log cabin in New York, Millard Fillmore worked on his father's farm and studied hard. He served in the House of Representatives for eight years before he unexpectedly became President after the death of Zachary Taylor.

FAST FACTS

13th President of the USA
Born: January 7, 1800
Died: March 8, 1874
Terms: 1850–1853 **Party:** Whig
First Lady: Abigail Powers
Vice President: Daniel D. Tompkins

FREE STATE

When President Taylor died suddenly, Vice President Fillmore took office, inheriting all the problems that were then being hotly debated. He backed the controversial Compromise of 1850, a set of five bills including one that would admit California as a free state and one that would abolish the slave trade in Washington, D.C. This would satisfy the Northern states, but it made the Southern states angry.

▼ *Many white abolitionists helped slaves to escape from the South to the North along the Underground Railroad.*

FUGITIVE SLAVE ACT

By 1850, thousands of slaves had escaped to the North by using a network of secret routes and safe houses known as the Underground Railroad. The Fugitive Slave Act, another part of the Compromise, allowed Southerners to recapture these slaves. Although the Southern states were happy with this, it made people in the North furious. The "compromise" wasn't working very well.

Fillmore was the last U.S. President to represent the Whig party.

Franklin Pierce 1853–1857

A New Englander from New Hampshire, Franklin Pierce studied law before entering politics, eventually becoming a senator. When he became President, the division in the Union seemed to have been resolved—but it turned out to be the calm before another storm.

TRAGEDY

Two months before Pierce entered the White House, he and his wife witnessed their 11-year-old son being killed in a train crash. The President and Mrs. Pierce—who disliked politics anyway—arrived in Washington, D.C., in a grief-stricken state.

◄ *Pierce shown shortly after his presidency in 1858.*

BLEEDING KANSAS

To try and pacify the South, Pierce signed the Kansas-Nebraska Act of 1854, which allowed new states to vote for slavery. Both Northerners and Southerners rushed into Kansas in a bid to control the area. The riots that broke out in "Bleeding Kansas" were a sign of the violence that would soon engulf the country in the **Civil War**.

RAILROAD LAND

President Pierce wanted a railroad built between Chicago and California, and offered Mexico $10 million for land in southern Arizona and New Mexico. More land meant reopening the question of slavery and yet more bitterness. However, the sale of the land went ahead.

FAST FACTS

14th President of the USA
Born: November 23, 1804
Died: October 8, 1869
Term: 1853–1857 **Party:** Democratic
First Lady: Jane Means Appleton
Vice President: William R. King

James Buchanan 1857–1861

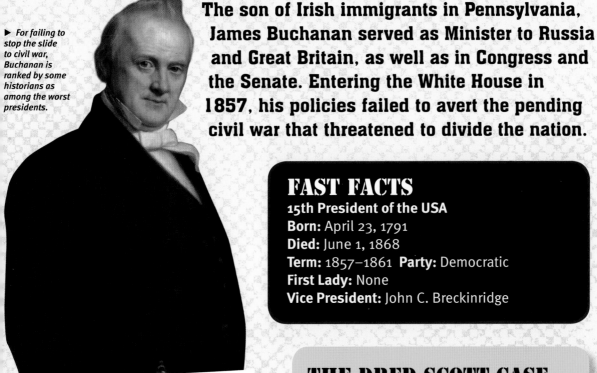

► *For failing to stop the slide to civil war, Buchanan is ranked by some historians as among the worst presidents.*

The son of Irish immigrants in Pennsylvania, James Buchanan served as Minister to Russia and Great Britain, as well as in Congress and the Senate. Entering the White House in 1857, his policies failed to avert the pending civil war that threatened to divide the nation.

FAST FACTS

15th President of the USA
Born: April 23, 1791
Died: June 1, 1868
Term: 1857–1861 **Party:** Democratic
First Lady: None
Vice President: John C. Breckinridge

▼ *John Brown and his men try to storm the arsenal at Harpers Ferry.*

THE DRED SCOTT CASE

In 1857, an enslaved man, Dred Scott, moved with his owner from a slave state to a free state where slavery was illegal. Scott tried to sue for his freedom but the U.S. Supreme Court ruled against him. The ruling denied any African American—free or enslaved—the right to citizenship. This angered many antislavery protesters in the North.

► *Dred Scott, an enslaved man, sued for his freedom at the Supreme Court in a landmark case.*

HARPERS FERRY

At the end of Buchanan's term, the country was clearly heading toward war. In 1859, a white abolitionist named John Brown tried—and failed—to start a slave uprising by leading a raid against a United States weapons arsenal at Harpers Ferry in Virginia.

After an ill-fated love affair, James Buchanan became the only President never to wed.

Abraham Lincoln 1861–1865

Having studied law, Abraham Lincoln's sense of justice served him well during the Civil War when he guided the Union to victory over the Southern states. The conflict ended with the preservation of the Union and abolition of slavery. He is one of the most famous of all presidents.

HONORABLE WORDS

Lincoln ran for senator in 1858. Although he lost, his eloquence led to him winning the Republican presidential nomination and the 1860 election. On November 19, 1863, in Pennsylvania, he delivered the Gettysburg Address, a speech reminding people that it was important to keep the Union together as a democracy, so that the "government of the people, by the people, for the people, shall not perish from the earth."

SOUTHERN SECESSION

Angered by President Lincoln's support for the abolition of slavery, the seven Southern "slave states" **seceded** from the Union and formed a Confederacy. When, in April 1861, Confederate forces attacked Fort Sumter in South Carolina, Lincoln sent 75,000 Union troops to defend it. The Civil War had begun.

▼ Confederate forces bombard Union troops in Fort Sumter, the action that started the Civil War.

◄ This iconic photograph of Lincoln was taken in 1863, when he was 54 years old.

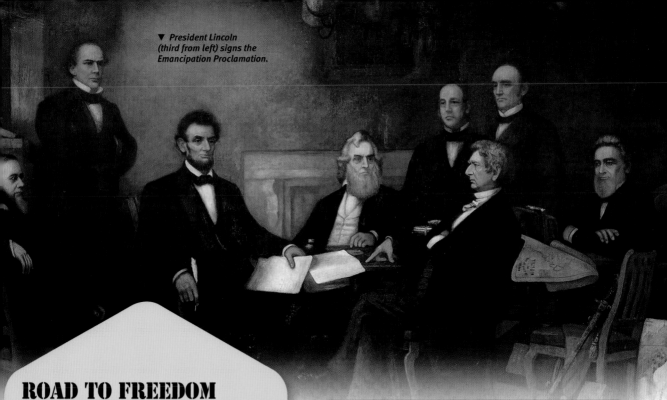

▼ President Lincoln (third from left) signs the Emancipation Proclamation.

ROAD TO FREEDOM

Determined to abolish slavery, Lincoln signed the landmark Emancipation Proclamation on January 1, 1863. At the stroke of a pen, he had changed the **federal** legal status of millions of enslaved people within the Confederacy from "slave" to "free." The abolition of slavery was enshrined in the 13th Amendment, which was passed by the Senate in April 1864.

FAST FACTS

16th President of the USA
Born: February 12, 1809
Died: April 15, 1865
Terms (two): 1861–1865 **Party:** Republican
First Lady: Mary Todd
Vice Presidents: Hannibal Hamlin 1861–1865, Andrew Johnson 1865

▲ This painting shows Confederate sympathizer John Wilkes Booth shooting President Lincoln.

UNTIMELY DEATH

The Civil War ended on April 9, 1865, but Lincoln did not have much time to enjoy the nation's peace. On April 14, the actor John Wilkes Booth shot and killed President Lincoln as he and his wife Mary watched a play at Ford's Theater in Washington, D.C.

Andrew Johnson 1865–1869

Born in North Carolina, Andrew Johnson served in the House of Representatives and the Senate before he became Vice President in 1865. The sudden death of Lincoln catapulted him into the presidency and the huge challenge of rebuilding a war-torn country.

Andrew Johnson

RECONSTRUCTION

President Johnson began the process of **Reconstruction**—the reforming of the Confederate states. People in the South who were willing to swear an oath of allegiance were pardoned, while cities and towns were rebuilt.

BIBLE

FAST FACTS

17th President of the USA
Born: December 29, 1808
Died: July 31, 1875
Term: 1865–1869 **Party:** Democratic
First Lady: Eliza McCardie
Vice President: None

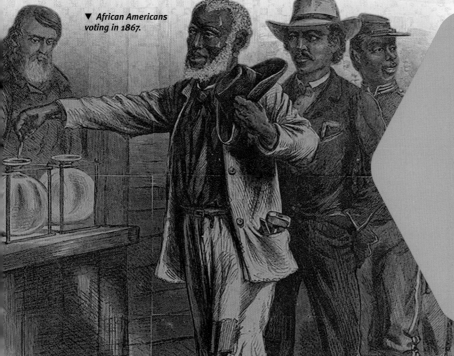

▼ *African Americans voting in 1867.*

AFRICAN AMERICAN RIGHTS

By December 1865, the 13th Amendment—which abolished slavery—had been adopted nationwide. But many states still tried to limit African Americans' freedom with "black codes," laws that kept former slaves in low-paid labor. The **Civil Rights** Act of 1866 and the 14th Amendment of 1868 made male African Americans official citizens, giving them the same legal rights as white citizens.

Ulysses S. Grant 1869–1877

As a boy Grant went to West Point military academy against his will, but still went on to become the Commanding General of the Union. He received the surrender of Confederate General Robert E. Lee, leading to the end of the Civil War. As President, he continued the Reconstruction.

15TH AMENDMENT

Even after the passing of the 13th and 14th amendments, many black people were still being prevented from voting in the South. So Grant oversaw the passing of the 15th amendment in 1870, which forbade states from denying someone the right to vote based on their race or color.

◀ Grant photographed during the final year of his presidency.

FAST FACTS

18th President of the USA
Born: April 27. 1822
Died: July 23, 1885
Terms (two): 1869–1877
Party: Republican
First Lady: Julia Boggs Dent
Vice Presidents: Schuyler Colfax 1869–1873, Henry Wilson 1873–1875

The "S" in his name didn't stand for anything—it was added as a mistake on a form.

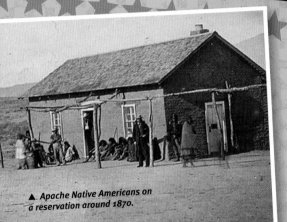

▲ Apache Native Americans on a reservation around 1870.

RESERVATIONS

President Grant worked to change policies toward Native Americans. He thought that housing them on reservations and helping them become farmers would help. But the land given to them was barren, and many ended up in extreme poverty.

Expansion and Power

As more states joined the Union, railroads were built to open the new lands to immigrants and prospectors. The end of the Apache Wars in 1886 allowed settlers to spread across the entire continent.

NEW STATES

In 1889, Montana, North Dakota, South Dakota, and Washington became states, followed by Idaho and Wyoming in 1890, Utah in 1896, and New Mexico and Arizona became states in 1912.

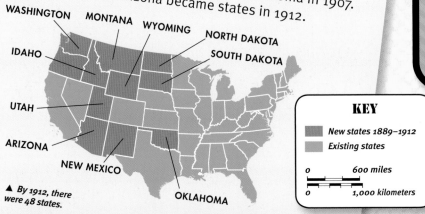

WASHINGTON MONTANA WYOMING NORTH DAKOTA SOUTH DAKOTA IDAHO UTAH ARIZONA NEW MEXICO OKLAHOMA

▲ By 1912, there were 48 states.

KEY

■ New states 1889–1912
■ Existing states

0   600 miles
0   1,000 kilometers

THE GILDED AGE

After the reforms of Reconstruction, America grew rapidly. New states were added, and the economy almost doubled in size. Attracted by the promise of a better life, waves of European immigrants arrived. Entrepreneurs such as John D. Rockefeller, Cornelius Vanderbilt, and Andrew Carnegie made fortunes from oil, railroad, and steel, and poured money into public works. The USA was becoming an industrial power.

▼ Innovative architect Frank Lloyd Wright designed his own home and studio in Oak Park, near Chicago, Illinois, in 1889.

BUILDING EVERYWHERE

A housing boom supported the growing U.S. population. Family houses were built by the thousands, reaching out from cities as new suburbs. Wealthy people sought brilliant architects such as Frank Furness, Frank Lloyd Wright, and Richard Morris Hunt to design amazing mansions, hotels, and public buildings in Philadelphia, Chicago, and New York.

KEY EVENTS

★ **SEPTEMBER 1881**
President Garfield is assassinated (see page 35).

★ **SEPTEMBER 1886**
Apache chief Geronimo surrenders, ending the Apache Wars in the Southwest (see page 37).

★ **OCTOBER 1889**
The Pan-American Conference is set up (see page 38).

★ **MAY 1894**
Pullman railroad workers go on strike (see page 39).

TRANSPORTATION NETWORKS

The growing nation needed a larger transportation network to make it run smoothly. Railroad lines were extended, and railroads became one of the largest employers in America. In 1870, construction started on the new Northern Pacific Railway, a transcontinental line that ran from the Great Lakes to the Pacific Ocean. The Panama Canal, built in 1904–1914, also helped make the United States a global power by allowing shipping trade from the Atlantic to the Pacific.

▶ *Huge steam trains carried passengers and freight along the Northern Pacific Railway. It had 6,800 miles of track.*

▲ The Northern Pacific Railway extended from Lake Superior in the east to the Pacific Ocean in the west.

APRIL 1898
The Spanish-American War begins (see page 41).

SEPTEMBER 1901
President McKinley is shot and dies (see page 41).

MAY 1904
Construction of the Panama Canal begins (see page 43).

FEBRUARY 1905
The U.S. National Forest Service is established (see page 42).

Rutherford B. Hayes 1877–1881

Rutherford B. Hayes

Born in Ohio, Rutherford B. Hayes fought in the Civil War, becoming a major general. After three terms as governor of Ohio, he won the presidential election by a single electoral vote. As President, he oversaw the end of Reconstruction.

FAST FACTS

19th President of the USA
Born: October 4, 1822
Died: January 17, 1893
Term: 1877–1881 **Party:** Republican
First Lady: Lucy Ware Webb
Vice President: William A. Wheeler

RAW DEAL

Hayes wanted to help African Americans who were still being discriminated against in the South. In 1877, he agreed to withdraw federal troops in the Southern states in return for their promise to protect African Americans' civil and voting rights. This promise, however, was soon broken.

JOBS BY MERIT

President Hayes appointed men to his Cabinet based on their ability, not their political background—he even chose one former Confederate. This attitude angered his fellow Republicans: They had helped him win the election, so they expected to be given the top government jobs.

▼ Hayes (center front) is shown sitting with his Cabinet.

In 1877, Alexander Graham Bell installed the first telephone in the White House.

James A. Garfield March–Sept. 1881

James A. Garfield had a humble early life. He worked to pay for his education, doing everything from teaching to driving canal boats. Eventually, he served in the Senate and Congress. In 1880, Garfield won the presidential election, and in his brief term set about reforming the civil service, boosting the navy, and cleaning up political **corruption**.

FAST FACTS

20th President of the USA
Born: November 19, 1831
Died: September 19, 1881
Term: 1881
Party: Republican
First Lady: Lucretia Rudolph
Vice President: Chester A. Arthur

PORT CONTROL

To tackle corruption in the New York Customs House, Garfield asserted federal control over the collection of import taxes at New York, the main entry port for goods into the USA. A political battle ensued with powerful New York senator Roscoe Conkling, but the President got his own way and Conkling resigned.

▼ In 1880, Garfield became the Republican Party's candidate for President, defeating former President General Ulysses S. Grant (right).

ASSASSINATION

Just 100 days after his term began, on July 2, 1881, President Garfield was shot down in a Washington railroad station by Charles J. Guiteau. The embittered assassin had not been offered the government job he wanted. Doctors tried to help the President, and Alexander Graham Bell even tried to find the bullet with his new metal detector, but Garfield died two months later.

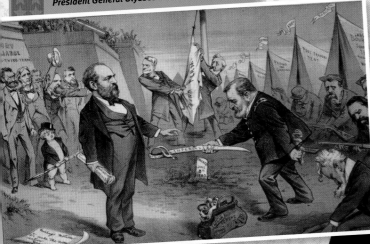

▶ Garfield sought to increase U.S. naval power during his short presidency.

Chester A. Arthur
1881–1885

Chester A. Arthur was born in Vermont. He rose to become the Collector of the Port of New York, a powerful post that led to his election as Vice President in 1880. In 1881, Arthur became President following Garfield's assassination. Continuing Garfield's reforms, Arthur's main achievement was the Pendleton Act of 1883, which ensured that civil servants were appointed on their ability, not their political affiliation.

EARLY CAREER

As a young lawyer in 1854, Chester A. Arthur defended Elizabeth Jennings, an African American who had refused to leave the white section of a Brooklyn streetcar. Jennings won the case but it took ten more years for New York's public transport to become fully **desegregated**.

◀ *Arthur made civil service reform the centerpiece of his presidency.*

FAST FACTS
21st President of the USA
Born: October 5, 1829
Died: November 18, 1886
Term: 1881–1885 **Party:** Republican
First Lady: Ellen Lewis Herndon
Vice President: None

IMMIGRATION BILL

In 1882, the President signed an act to prevent any "convict, lunatic, idiot, or person unable to take care of himself or herself" from entering the USA. It also charged each immigrant a 50-cent duty!

$

President Arthur dressed elegantly and threw lavish parties at the White House.

Grover Cleveland
1885–1889

Born in New Jersey, Grover Cleveland was a lawyer and Governor of New York before becoming President. He is the only President to have been elected twice with a gap between terms. Noted for his honesty and integrity, he tirelessly fought corruption. When Chief Geronimo surrendered in 1886, the Apache Wars ended and Cleveland promoted the assimilation of Native Americans.

▶ Portrait of Cleveland taken in 1903 after his second term in office.

President Cleveland opened the Statue of Liberty, a gift from France, in 1886.

FAST FACTS

22nd President of the USA
Born: March 18, 1837
Died: June 24, 1908
Terms (two): 1885–1889 & 1893–1897
Party: Democratic
First Lady: Frances Folsom
Vice President: Thomas A. Hendricks

NO FAVORS

In his aim to fight corruption, President Cleveland was determined not to favor any particular groups for special treatment. He went so far as to refuse pensions to disabled Civil War veterans, and when Texan farmers were suffering from extreme drought, he failed to pass a bill that would give them money for seeds.

Frances Folsom

WHITE WEDDING

Grover Cleveland became the first President to wed at the White House when he married Frances Folsom in June 1886. A recent graduate and 27 years younger than Cleveland, Frances reignited interest in the administration and became a very popular First Lady.

Benjamin Harrison 1889–1893

Benjamin Harrison was born into a political family in Ohio; his grandfather was the nation's ninth president, William H. Harrison. Benjamin became a brilliant lawyer and practiced in Indianapolis. In the 1880s, he served in the Senate, supporting the rights of Native Americans, veterans, and homesteaders. His presidency saw many changes to foreign and domestic policies.

◀ *The unpopularity of his import tariffs and $1 billion budget saw Harrison voted out of office after just one term.*

FAST FACTS

23rd President of the USA
Born: August 20, 1833
Died: March 13, 1901
Term: 1889–1893 **Party:** Republican
First Lady: Caroline Lavinia Scott
Vice President: Levi P. Morton

POLICY POWER

Congress allocated $1 billion to improve the country and expand the navy to protect American shipping. A high **tariff** was put on imports to force people to buy U.S.-made goods, and a federal bill was introduced to limit the power of huge companies. The Pan-American Conference of 1889, intended to promote international relations, was used to open Latin American markets to U.S. trade.

PROTECTING CIVIL RIGHTS

Frederick Douglass (below)—the renowned writer, abolitionist, statesman, and former slave—was made minister to Haiti by the President. At home, President Harrison backed bills intended to make sure that Southern states allowed African Americans to vote.

▼ *The USS* Columbia, *a navy cruiser built during Harrison's administration.*

President Harrison let his grandchildren keep a goat on the White House lawn!

Grover Cleveland 1893–1897

When Grover Cleveland returned for a second term as President after a four-year gap, the country was in the grips of an **economic depression**. Unfortunately, the President's policies did little to help the country get back on its feet.

Cleveland's 1893 Cabinet

THE PANIC OF 1893

In 1893, wheat prices fell, railroad companies went bankrupt, and several banks collapsed. Government gold reserves fell so low that the President was forced to borrow supplies from the financier J. P. Morgan. Many people blamed the situation on a policy called the Sherman Silver Purchase Act, which had driven down the price of silver. Cleveland reversed the act, but the economic problems continued.

FAST FACTS

24th President of the USA
Born: March 18, 1837
Died: June 24, 1908
Terms (two): 1885–1889 & 1893–1897
Party: Democratic
First Lady: Frances Folsom
Vice President: Adlai E. Stevenson

▶ *Eugene V. Debs, the leader of the American Railway Union.*

PULLMAN RAILROAD STRIKE

Thousands of strikes and massive unemployment came as a result of the depression. In 1894, around 150,000 railroad workers came to Chicago to support a strike by the Pullman Car workers. President Cleveland sent in federal troops to break up the strike, which caused many people to turn against him and the Democratic party.

◀ *Federal troops face strikers during the Pullman Railroad Strike of 1894.*

William McKinley 1897–1901

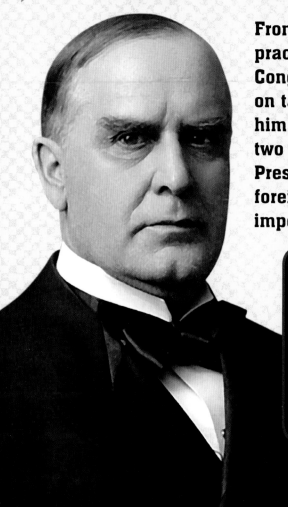

From Niles, Ohio, William McKinley practiced law and later entered Congress, where he became an expert on tariffs. His likable personality made him popular with voters, and he served two terms as Governor of Ohio. As President, he dealt extensively with foreign policy and tariffs, taxing imported goods to protect U.S. industry.

FAST FACTS

25th President of the USA
Born: January 29, 1843
Died: September 14, 1901
Terms (two): 1897–1901
Party: Republican
First Lady: Ida Saxton
Vice Presidents: Garret A. Hobart 1897–1899, Theodore Roosevelt 1901

◄ McKinley was the third U.S. President to be assassinated.

FIRST LADY IDA

Before she married William McKinley in 1871, Ida Saxton worked at—and sometimes managed—her father's bank in Ohio. When she became First Lady, Mrs. McKinley had lost her only two children to illnesses and suffered from epilepsy. But this did not stop her from advising the President on speeches, backing women's suffrage and African-American education, and promoting the arts.

Ida Saxton

SPANISH-AMERICAN WAR

In 1898, Cuban rebel forces were fighting a war to be free of Spanish colonial rule. President McKinley had hoped for a peaceful resolution but declared war after outrage from Americans at the suffering of the Cubans and the explosion of the U.S.S. *Maine* in Havana Harbor. The Spanish-American War lasted just 100 days, with Spain's aging ships proving no match for the modern U.S. Navy.

▲ U.S troops face the enemy from a trench during the short-lived Spanish-American War.

ISLAND TERRITORIES

After winning the Spanish-American War, the United States vowed to protect Cuba, but in fact continued to occupy the island. It also took control of the former Spanish territories of Puerto Rico, Guam, and the Philippines, establishing itself as a growing world power.

ASSASSINATION NO. 3

Just months into his second term, President McKinley was at the Pan-American Exposition in Buffalo when an anarchist shot him twice at close range on September 6, 1901. He died eight days later.

▶ McKinley's assassin, Leon Czolgosz, shot the President with his gun hidden in a handkerchief.

Theodore Roosevelt 1901–1909

Theodore Roosevelt

In 1898, Theodore "Teddy" Roosevelt led a U.S. Volunteer unit—the "Rough Riders"—during the Spanish-American War. He returned a hero and was elected governor of New York and then Vice President. When McKinley was assassinated, Roosevelt became a hugely popular leader, focusing on conservation, social justice, and foreign policy.

FAST FACTS

26th President of the USA
Born: October 27, 1858
Died: January 6, 1919
Terms (two): 1901–1909
Party: Republican
First Lady: Edith Kermit Carow
Vice President: Charles W. Fairbanks

CONSERVATION WORK

President Roosevelt believed it was important that the nation's wilderness be preserved for future generations, so he created the United States Forest Service. Its 230 million acres of public land include 150 national forests and five national parks, such as Yosemite and Mesa Verde.

▼ Yosemite National Park, which Roosevelt brought under government control in 1906.

A NEW CANAL

In 1904, construction began on the Panama Canal, a shortcut between North and South America cutting through Panama, which had just been liberated from Spain. This huge engineering feat took years to build and cost the United States $375 million. Thousands of workers died during its construction.

Roosevelt felt that the government should help American people and prevent large companies from taking over small companies. In 1902, he tested this idea by intervening in a coal strike in Pennsylvania. Known as the "Square Deal," it was the first domestic policy of its kind. Roosevelt also passed the Pure Food and Drug Act in 1906 to regulate food and drug safety.

▲ A modern cargo ship entering a lock on the canal.

▲ Ships at the Atlanic entrance to the Panama Canal in 1913, a year before it opened.

FAMILY

In 1884, Theodore Roosevelt's mother and first wife both died on the same day. He spent the next two years at his cattle ranch in North Dakota recovering from the tragedy. Here, he developed his views on conservation. In 1896, he married Edith Kermit Carow—together, they brought up their five children and daughter Alice from his first marriage. The family was followed by the press, who loved to hear about their hikes, picnics, and storytelling nights.

◄ Theodore Roosevelt with his wife Edith Carow and their five children.

30

William Howard Taft 1909–1913

Born in Cincinnati, Ohio, William Howard Taft was the son of a respected judge. He studied at Yale and Cincinnati Law School before practicing law. In 1904, Taft became Secretary of War in the Roosevelt Administration, which led to his running for president on the Republican ticket in 1908. During his term as President, Taft made many advances in federal law.

RELUCTANT PRESIDENT

President Taft was not happy in the White House—he preferred to work in law and had run for office only because his wife, Helen Herron Taft, had big ambitions for him. A naturally conservative politician, Taft often had to defend himself against progressive Republicans, who bad-mouthed him for not following the former President Roosevelt's policies.

◀ *Taft takes the telephone call telling him that he is the Republican candidate for President.*

Helen Herron

FAST FACTS

27th President of the USA
Born: September 15, 1857
Died: March 8, 1930
Term: 1909–1913 **Party:** Republican
First Lady: Helen Herron
Vice President: James S. Sherman

DOLLAR DIPLOMACY

Anxious to expand foreign trade, President Taft set up "dollar diplomacy," a program that encouraged U.S. investments in places like Central and South America and the Far East. He sent government officials to foreign countries to sell products such as military and industrial equipment.

▲ Taft with his wife (left) at a baseball game in 1910.

ACHIEVEMENTS

As he was considered a poor successor to Roosevelt, many politicians did not notice that, during his term, President Taft backed 80 suits to help smaller companies stay in business against larger ones. He also helped establish a federal income tax, set up a postal savings system, and backed the direct election of senators.

▼ Taft in the 1920s, dressed in his U.S. Supreme Court robes.

JUSTICE AT LAST

When his term ended, William Howard Taft worked at Yale as a law professor. Then, in 1921, he was made Chief Justice of the Supreme Court, the job he had always wanted. He served there until just before his death in 1930 and is the only person to have been both President and Chief Justice.

The World at War

During the 20th century, two catastrophic World Wars began in Europe. The United States attempted to stay out of them. However, the global reach of the conflicts made American neutrality impossible and the nation was twice drawn into the fighting.

WORLD WAR I

In June 1914, World War I broke out in Europe. President Wilson tried to keep the United States out of the conflict, sending supplies and money to its allies, Britain, France, and Russia, in their fight against Germany, Austria-Hungary, and the Ottoman Empire. By 1917, Germany was attacking U.S. shipping and encouraging Mexico to reclaim Texas, Arizona, and New Mexico. The threat to the United States was clear, and it joined the war. In 1918, Germany was defeated. The conflict had claimed millions of lives.

▶ *U.S. soldiers throw grenades at Austrian troops from their trenches during World War I.*

KEY EVENTS

★ **APRIL 6, 1917**
The United States enters World War I (see page 48).

★ **AUGUST 26, 1920**
Women are granted the right to vote nationwide (see page 48).

★ **OCTOBER 24, 1929**
The stock market crashes; the Great Depression begins (see page 51).

★ **MAY 18, 1933**
President Franklin D. Roosevelt's New Deal is signed (see page 52).

LEAGUE OF NATIONS

After World War I, President Wilson helped create the League of Nations, a body dedicated to solving international conflicts through diplomacy. But Congress refused to give its approval and the United States didn't become a member. Wilson toured America in an attempt to win support, but, exhausted, he had a massive stroke and almost died.

◄ President Wilson (right) meets with the leaders of Britain, France, and Italy after World War I.

WORLD WAR II

When German dictator Adolf Hitler invaded Poland in 1939, Great Britain and France declared war on Germany, and World War II began. President Roosevelt kept the United States out of the war initially. But after Japan attacked the U.S. naval base at Pearl Harbor in 1941, the USA joined the conflict. Germany surrendered in May 1945. A few months later, after the United States dropped atomic bombs on Hiroshima and also Nagasaki, Japan surrendered.

◄ U.S. troops approach the beaches of France on D-Day, June 6, 1944, in an effort to liberate German-occupied France.

DECEMBER 7, 1941
The United States joins Allied nations in World War II (see page 53).

AUGUST 1945
Atomic bombs are dropped on Japan (see page 54).

AUGUST 15, 1945
World War II ends (see page 54).

APRIL 4, 1949
The NATO treaty is signed (see page 55).

Woodrow Wilson 1913–1921

Woodrow Wilson

Elected President in 1912, Wilson initially opposed entry of the United States into World War I, before he changed his mind in 1917. During his term, he also passed acts for controlling banks, credit, and money that are still used today.

FAST FACTS

28th President of the USA
Born: December 28, 1856
Died: February 3, 1924
Terms (two): 1913–1921 **Party:** Democratic
First Lady: Ellen Axson Wilson (died 1914), Edith Bolling Galt
Vice President: Thomas R. Marshall

VOTES FOR WOMEN

The influence of the suffragette campaigns—and in particular the vital contribution of women to the war effort—meant that the issue of votes for women could no longer be ignored. In 1920, toward the end of Wilson's presidency, the 19th Amendment was passed, granting the vote to women.

EUROPEAN WAR

Having witnessed the awful aftermath of the Civil War as a child, President Wilson wanted to avoid having the USA fight in World War I, though he supported the cause of the Allies. But when German submarines began attacking American ships in 1917, Congress declared war on Germany, and U.S. troops helped hasten the Allied victory in 1918.

▼ *Two U.S. soldiers head toward the enemy in World War I.*

Warren G. Harding
1921–1923

As a young man, Harding ran a newspaper popular with politicians, which helped him become a senator in 1914. When running for President, he gave speeches about returning the country to "normalcy." But when he won by a huge landslide, President Harding admitted to colleagues that the job was beyond him—and his term exposed his shortcomings.

FAST FACTS

29th President of the USA
Born: November 2, 1865
Died: August 2, 1923
Term: 1921–1923 **Party:** Republican
First Lady: Florence Kling De Wolfe
Vice President: Calvin Coolidge

DOMESTIC DEALS

President Harding was well-liked by Republican members of Congress because he signed most of their bills. These included acts to end wartime controls, cut taxes, raise tariffs, and place strict controls on immigration. In 1921, he also signed an act for women to receive better prenatal care.

▶ Immigrants arriving in New York in the early 20th century—their numbers were greatly reduced by Harding's policies.

TEAPOT DOME SCANDAL

The President knew that someone in his administration was accepting bribes from oil companies but was unsure what to do about it and so kept quiet. Eventually, an investigation sent a member of his Cabinet to jail. Known as the Teapot Dome Scandal, the episode severely damaged Harding's administration.

▶ Harding won 61 percent of the vote in the 1920 presidential election.

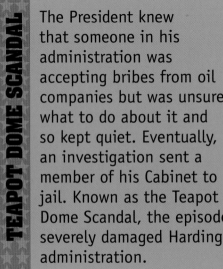

Calvin Coolidge
1923–1929

Born in Vermont, Calvin Coolidge started his career in law before moving into politics, rising to become Vice President. When President Harding died, he took over the presidency. The "Roaring Twenties" were a time of great prosperity for many Americans, and Coolidge's policies aimed to keep things that way.

JUST SAY NO

Coolidge worked to limit the government's involvement in big business and to cut income taxes: Only the wealthiest people paid them. Aiming to keep federal spending low, he vetoed bills to aid struggling farmers and to develop cheap electricity, which would have helped people in poor areas.

◄ Coolidge's policies laid the ground for economic turmoil.

FAST FACTS

30th President of the USA
Born: July 4, 1872
Died: January 5, 1933
Terms (two): 1923–1928 **Party:** Republican
First Lady: Grace Anna Goodhue
Vice President: Charles G. Dawes

▲ Coolidge signed the Indian Citizenship Act in 1924, which finally granted citizenship to the country's Native Americans.

GOOD PUBLICITY

Understanding the power of the press, President Coolidge spoke at hundreds of press conferences. He was photographed alongside Native Americans and wearing farmer's overalls, to show he was working for the people. In reality, he did little to solve the United States' economic problems.

In 1924, Coolidge delivered the first presidential address to be broadcast on radio.

Herbert Hoover 1929–1933

Born into a Quaker family in Iowa, Herbert Hoover studied geology at Stanford University. He became a successful mining engineer and worked for the U.S. government feeding war-torn Europe. As President, Hoover tried to lead the country out of the worst financial downturn it had ever known.

THE GREAT DEPRESSION

At his inauguration in March 1929, Hoover believed the nation had conquered poverty. But on October 24, the stock market crashed, billions of dollars were lost, and the country went into the Great Depression (1929–1939). Businesses crumbled, leading to widespread unemployment, hunger, and desperation for millions.

FREE SOUP

▲ Unemployed men line up outside a soup kitchen in Chicago at the height of the Great Depression.

TOO LITTLE, TOO LATE

Hoover backed a range of programs designed to improve the economy, including funding public works and giving subsidies to farmers. But the situation continued to worsen, and many blamed Hoover for not doing enough to stop the Depression.

FAST FACTS

31st President of the USA
Born: August 10, 1874
Died: October 20, 1964
Term: 1929–1933
Party: Democratic
First Lady: Lou Henry
Vice President: Charles Curtis

◄ Herbert Hoover campaigning during the 1928 presidential election.

Franklin D. Roosevelt 1933–1945

When Franklin D. Roosevelt (FDR) took office in 1933, the United States was in the grip of the Great Depression, a time when thirteen million people were out of work and many banks had shut down. Assisted by his wife, Eleanor, President Roosevelt aimed to set the country on its feet again with his innovative policies and unfailing optimism.

◀ *A portrait of FDR sitting in the Oval Office at the White House. Roosevelt suffered from polio, which left him partially paralyzed.*

Roosevelt remains the only president to have served more than two terms.

NEW DEAL

From 1933, President Roosevelt introduced the New Deal, a series of measures and public works that would tackle unemployment and poverty. These included programs to help farmers, build dams, construct new buildings, and grant loans. FDR also backed the Social Security Act, signed on August 14, 1935, which aimed to protect people against poverty.

FAST FACTS
32nd President of the USA
Born: January 30, 1882
Died: April 12, 1945
Terms (four): 1933–1945 **Party:** Democratic
First Lady: Anna Eleanor Roosevelt
Vice Presidents: John N. Garner 1933–1941, Henry A. Wallace 1941–1945, Harry S. Truman 1945

WARTIME LEADER

During the early days of World War II, Roosevelt's government sent ships, supplies, and equipment to Great Britain to help in the struggle against Nazi Germany. However, following the surprise Japanese attack on Pearl Harbor, Congress declared war on both Germany and Japan. Throughout World War II, Roosevelt played a key role, along with Josef Stalin and Winston Churchill, in guiding the allies to victory.

▼ *U.S. battleships burning after the Japanese attack on Pearl Harbor in December 1941.*

From 1933–1944, President Roosevelt gave a series of radio talks called "fireside chats." His cheerful voice explaining his policies did much to endear him to the American public and eased people's fears during the Great Depression and World War II.

GROUNDBREAKING FIRST LADY

Eleanor Roosevelt understood the social conditions of the Depression and became very active as First Lady, holding press conferences, traveling across the USA, and giving radio broadcasts and lectures. Later in life, she became a spokesperson for the United Nations.

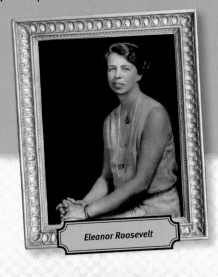

Eleanor Roosevelt

SUDDEN DEATH

On April 12, 1945, President Roosevelt was staying at his beloved "Little White House" in Warm Springs, Georgia, when he suffered a fatal brain hemorrhage while having his portrait painted. The nation mourned one of its most popular leaders ever.

Harry S. Truman 1945–1953

▶ Truman in 1945, after the end of World War II.

Truman was captain of an artillery unit in World War I and by 1934, had become a senator. Chosen by Franklin D. Roosevelt to be his Vice President, Truman became President when FDR died suddenly in 1945. Truman took over the role at one of the most crucial moments in history. He had to make some tough decisions about how to end World War II. His term also saw the early stages of the standoff between the United States and the Soviet Union.

FAST FACTS

33rd President of the USA
Born: May 8, 1884
Died: December 26, 1972
Terms (two): 1945–1953
Party: Democratic
First Lady: Elizabeth Wallace
Vice President: Alban W. Barkley

▲ Truman (center) meets the leaders of the UK, Clement Atlee (left), and the Soviet Union, Josef Stalin (right), at the Potsdam conference at the end of the war.

DEADLY BOMBS

World War II in Europe officially ended in May 1945. The United States asked Japan to surrender, but it refused. So President Truman and his advisors made the difficult decision to drop atomic bombs on the Japanese cities of Hiroshima and Nagasaki. The bombs left 100,000 people dead, and twice as many died later from radiation poisoning. Japan finally surrendered in August 1945.

In 1948, President Truman signed an order to end **segregation** in the U.S. armed forces and civil service. Executive Order 9981 states that there will be "equality of treatment and opportunity for all persons in the armed services without regard to race, color, religion, or national origin."

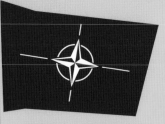

MILITARY ALLIANCE

President Truman and other Western leaders negotiated a military treaty for mutual protection. The North Atlantic Treaty Organization, or NATO, was established in 1949.

▼ *A U.S. tank crew keeps watch during the Korean War in 1950.*

KOREAN WAR

In June 1950, North Korea's **Communist** government attacked South Korea, an ally of the United States. President Truman acted quickly, sending in U.S.-led United Nations forces to help push the North Koreans back to the border of China. China, assisted by the Soviet Union, then entered the war fighting for North Korea against U.S. forces.

38

The Space Race

By the 1950s, the United States' rivalry with the Soviet Union had moved into space. Fears that its technology was lagging behind prompted the USA to invest billions of dollars in a program to a put a man on the Moon.

▲ *View of the Earth "rising" above the Moon taken by the crew of Apollo 8.*

EARLY SPACE

In October 1957, the Soviet Union caused panic in the United States by putting Sputnik, the world's first artificial satellite, into orbit. In response, President Dwight D. Eisenhower established NASA—the National Aeronautics and Space Administration—in 1958. Then in April 1961, a Russian, Yuri Gagarin, made the first manned space flight. Now the race was on: Who would put a human on the Moon first, the United States or the Soviet Union? This competition stimulated a rapid growth of space technology in both countries.

▶ *Yuri Gagarin became a global celebrity when his spacecraft orbited the Earth in 1961.*

KEY EVENTS

★ **JULY 27, 1953**
The Korean War ends (see page 58).

★ **OCTOBER 1, 1958**
NASA begins operations (see above).

★ **SEPTEMBER 4, 1957**
U.S. troops enforce civil rights in Little Rock (see page 59).

★ **OCTOBER 16–28, 1962**
The Cuban Missile Crisis (see page 60).

► President Kennedy makes his historic speech to Congress, committing the USA to landing a man on the Moon.

MAN ON THE MOON

The Apollo program continued with further missions. On July 20, 1969, President Kennedy's goal was realized when astronauts Neil Armstrong and Edwin "Buzz" Aldrin became the first humans to set foot on the Moon during the Apollo 11 mission. The whole world watched on TV screens, captivated, as Armstrong said, "one small step for a man, one giant leap for mankind." NASA continued the Apollo program until 1972.

JFK'S CHALLENGE

On May 25, 1961, at a special session of Congress, President John F. Kennedy made a bold statement: The United States would put a man on the Moon by the end of the decade. Kennedy's successor, President Lyndon B. Johnson, continued the space program, and in 1968, the first astronauts orbited the Moon in Apollo 8—an amazing achievement.

▼ Buzz Aldrin peforms an experiment on the Moon during the first lunar landing in 1969.

JULY 2, 1964
The Civil Rights Act of 1964 is signed (see page 63).

JULY 27, 1964
President Johnson sends 5,000 troops to South Vietnam (see page 63).

JULY 20, 1969
The USA lands the first astronauts on the Moon (see above).

APRIL 29, 1974
The USA evacuates its final personnel from Vietnam (see page 64).

Dwight D. Eisenhower
1953–1961

Eisenhower had an illustrious military career that included commanding the Allied landings on D-Day during World War II. He returned to the USA a war hero and this reputation helped him to become President by a huge majority. His term was spent dealing with the **Cold War**, civil rights, and the construction of 41,000 miles of interstate highways.

Dwight D. Eisenhower

KOREAN WAR ENDS

On July 27, 1953, President Eisenhower and leaders from China, North Korea, and South Korea signed a truce ending the three-year-long Korean War. But the United States' relationship with China and the Soviet Union was left strained.

FAST FACTS

34th President of the USA
Born: October 14, 1890
Died: March 28, 1969
Terms (two): 1953–1961 **Party:** Republican
First Lady: Mamie Geneva Doud
Vice President: Richard M. Nixon

▼ *Eisenhower talks to U.S. troops before D-Day.*

Both Alaska and Hawaii became states in 1959 during Eisenhower's second term.

▲ Under Eisenhower, the United States used high-flying planes, such as this U2, to spy on Soviet military activities.

COLD WAR THREAT

By the early 1950s, the USA and the Soviet Union had both developed hydrogen bombs, and people were worried that if they were used, destruction on a global scale would follow. The hostile relationship between the U.S.-led Western countries and the Soviet Union and its allies was known as the Cold War. Eisenhower tried but was unable to make a pact with the Soviet leader Nikita Khrushchev to limit weapons testing.

STUDENTS DESEGREGATED

In 1954, a civil rights act was passed to end segregation in U.S. schools, meaning that African-American students were able to study at white schools. But in 1957, an angry crowd tried to stop nine African-American students from going to a white high school in Little Rock, Arkansas. President Eisenhower sent in federal troops to make sure that they could attend school safely.

HEART ATTACK

In 1955, Eisenhower suffered a heart attack during his first term. Despite recovering, he considered not standing for re-election, but he later changed his mind after a health check by his doctors.

◀ U.S. troops accompany the "Little Rock Nine" to school in 1957.

John F. Kennedy 1961–1963

Born into an influential, wealthy family, John F. Kennedy was educated at Harvard University. After returning from World War II a hero, he quickly worked his way up through politics, becoming a congressman in 1946 and a U.S. senator for Massachusetts in 1952. Despite many undisclosed health problems, Kennedy won the presidential election in 1961.

FAST FACTS

35th President of the USA
Born: May 29, 1917
Died: November 22, 1963
Term: 1961–1963 **Party:** Democratic
First Lady: Jacqueline Lee Bouvier
Vice President: Lyndon B. Johnson

▶ *Kennedy commanded a patrol boat in the Pacific during World War II.*

▲ *A U.S. Navy plane flies alongside a Soviet cargo ship carrying military equipment bound for Cuba.*

CUBAN CRISIS

In October 1962, U.S. reconnaissance aircraft spotted Soviet nuclear missiles on Cuba, just 90 miles from the coast of Florida. The U.S. government started a blockade of Cuba to stop more missiles and supplies from reaching the island. Over 13 days, from October 16–28, tensions were high and the world came close to a nuclear war, before the two sides reached a deal.

MOON QUEST

In 1961, President Kennedy and Congress decided that America would put a man on the Moon by the end of the 1960s. This space program would cost $22 billion and present an enormous technical challenge. On February 20, 1962, the "Space Race" began when Friendship 7, with astronaut John Glenn on board, became the first U.S.-manned flight to orbit Earth.

CIVIL RIGHTS FIGHT

In the early 1960s, there remained severe prejudice against African Americans, especially in the South. In June 1963, President Kennedy proposed a bill to Congress that would strengthen the civil rights of African Americans. On August 28, 1963, a civil rights activist named Dr. Martin Luther King, Jr. led a peaceful protest in Washington, D.C., to publicize the need for racial equality. In front of 250,000 people, Dr. King gave his famous "I have a dream" speech where he hoped that people would be judged by their character and not by the color of their skin.

▲ *Dr. Martin Luther King, Jr. delivers his famous speech in Washington, D.C.*

TRAGIC END

On November 22, 1963, on the streets of Dallas, Texas, the President and Mrs. Kennedy were riding in an open car, when shots were fired, fatally wounding the President. The world was stunned. It is thought that Lee Harvey Oswald fired the shot, but he himself was killed the next day by Jack Ruby on live television. Conspiracy theories still attempt to explain who was behind the assassination.

▼ *President Kennedy and his wife, Jackie, riding through Dallas, Texas, moments before the assassination.*

Lyndon B. Johnson 1963–1969

Born in Texas, Lyndon B. Johnson ("LBJ") became Vice President in 1961, before becoming President following Kennedy's death. As President, he worked to improve life for all Americans, launching programs in favor of civil rights and to combat poverty. He also had to deal with an unpopular war.

◄ *Johnson served in the navy during World War II.*

FAST FACTS

36th President of the USA
Born: August 27, 1908
Died: January 22, 1973
Terms (two): 1963–1969 **Party:** Democratic
First Lady: Claudia Alta "Lady Bird" Taylor
Vice President: Hubert H. Humphrey

▲ *Johnson takes the presidential oath next to President Kennedy's widow, Jacqueline (right).*

SWEARING IN

On November 22, 1963, an hour after President Kennedy was assassinated, Vice President Lyndon B. Johnson was hastily sworn in as President on board *Air Force One*. The brief ceremony was witnessed by Mrs. Kennedy, Mrs. Johnson, and government aides, with JFK's body on board. It was a dramatic entrance to the White House.

Johnson spent much of his early career teaching students from poor backgrounds.

VIETNAM WAR

The collapse of French colonial rule in Vietnam at the end of World War II led to fighting between communist forces to the north and the South Vietnam government. American military advisors had been helping South Vietnam since the 1950s, but President Johnson sent more U.S. troops in 1964 to fight the spread of communism. The escalation of the war in the following years sparked a wave of protests at home: People felt America should not become involved. LBJ's popularity suffered, and he did not run for another term in 1968.

▲ In 1967, people protest against the Vietnam War in Washington, D.C.

▲ Johnson meets with civil rights leaders, including Martin Luther King, Jr. (left), prior to the passing of the Civil Rights Act in 1964.

RIGHTS FOR ALL

President Johnson approved the landmark Civil Rights Act of 1964, which banned discrimination based on race, color, religion, or sex. It protected African Americans' right to vote and ended segregation at school and work, and in public places.

THE GREAT SOCIETY

President Johnson wanted to turn America into a "Great Society," one in which everyone was equal, educated, and healthy. In 1965, his Great Society program included bills to boost education, fight poverty, renew urban areas, and prevent crime. It also promoted conservation and created Medicare—health insurance for those over 65.

Richard M. Nixon
1969–1974

Richard Nixon served as a U.S. Navy lieutenant in World War II, before becoming Vice President in 1953 and President in 1969. One of his first acts was to end the Vietnam draft, which had forced men to fight in an unpopular war.

Richard Nixon

PATH TO PEACE

In 1972, President Nixon visited Moscow and Beijing on a quest to make the world more stable. His talks with Soviet leader Leonid Brezhnev resulted in a treaty to place limits on the use of nuclear weapons. He spoke to Chinese leaders Mao Zedong and Zhou Enlai about the war in Vietnam and, in 1973, agreed to end American involvement in Vietnam.

▼ *President Nixon and Chinese Premier Zhou Enlai raise a toast during their historic meeting in 1972.*

FAST FACTS

37th President of the USA
Born: January 9, 1913
Died: April 22, 1994
Terms (two): 1969–1974
Party: Republican
First Lady: Thelma "Pat" Ryan
Vice Presidents: Spiro Agnew 1969–1973, Gerald Ford 1973–1974

SCANDAL & RESIGNATION

The Nixon Administration ended in scandal. The president's staff were found to have broken into Democratic party offices at the Watergate Hotel in Washington, D.C., to wiretap political opponents. Recordings of Nixon trying to cover up the affair left people in no doubt as to his involvement. On August 8, 1974, Nixon became the only U.S. president to resign.

PRIVACY LAW

The Privacy Act of 1974 was a new law that gave Americans more privacy. It meant that federal agencies had to be more open and fair about the collection and use of people's personal data.

Gerald Ford 1974–1977

In 1974, when President Nixon resigned, Vice President Gerald Ford took office without being elected. A former university football star and long-time congressman, his renowned honesty served him well through the difficult tasks he faced: controlling inflation, boosting a depressed economy, and maintaining world peace.

FAST FACTS

38th President of the USA
Born: July 14, 1913
Died: December 26, 2006
Term: 1974–77 **Party:** Republican
First Lady: Elizabeth Anne "Betty" Bloomer
Vice President: Nelson Rockefeller

◀ *President Ford assures Egyptian leader Anwar Sadat of America's good intentions.*

MIDDLE EASTERN TALKS

Anxious to prevent a war in the Middle East, President Ford provided aid both to Egypt and Israel. This persuaded the two countries to accept an interim truce agreement in 1975.

FAILED ASSASSINS

President Ford survived two assassination attempts in 1975. On September 5, Lynette Fromme tried to shoot him as he went to shake her hand in a crowd. She later claimed she was trying to draw attention to environmental pollution. Then, on September 22, Sara Jane Moore shot at Ford; she served 32 years in prison for the crime.

In 1930, Ford was selected to play football for the Grand Rapids City League in Michigan.

44

International Diplomacy

▶ *U.S. President Obama discusses international affairs with South Korean President Lee Myung-bak in Seoul, 2010.*

Since the end of the Cold War, the United States has had a unique diplomatic influence as the world's only superpower. Today, however, China's increasing military power and Russia's renewed strength are causing a shift in the balance of world power.

▲ *People chip apart the Berlin Wall, a notorious symbol of the Cold War, to sell as souvenirs.*

THE COLD WAR ENDS

In 1991, the breakup of the Soviet Union marked the end of the Cold War. The 55-year threat of hostility between the Soviet countries and U.S.-led powers was over. In Germany, the Berlin Wall, which had closed off Communist East Berlin to democratic West Berlin, opened up in 1989–90 and was dismantled, symbolizing a new era for Europe and the world.

▶ *Soldiers from the USA and France take part in a joint anti-terrorism exercise in 2004.*

KEY EVENTS

★ **SEPTEMBER 17, 1978**
Camp David Accords (see page 69).

★ **NOVEMBER 4, 1979**
Iran hostage crisis begins (see page 69).

★ **DECEMBER 8, 1987**
Reagan and Gorbachev sign a nuclear weapons treaty (see page 70).

★ **DECEMBER 1991**
The Cold War ends (see page 71).

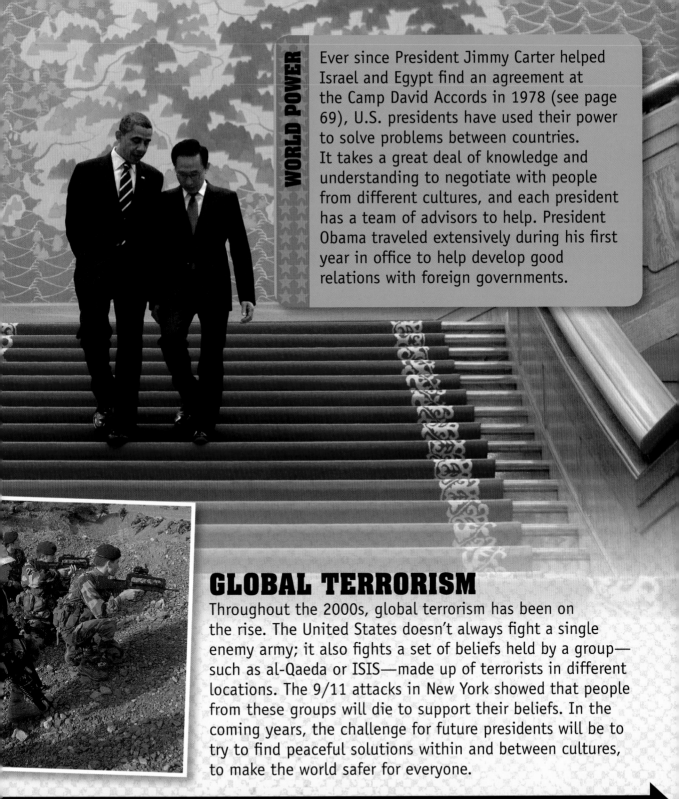

Ever since President Jimmy Carter helped Israel and Egypt find an agreement at the Camp David Accords in 1978 (see page 69), U.S. presidents have used their power to solve problems between countries. It takes a great deal of knowledge and understanding to negotiate with people from different cultures, and each president has a team of advisors to help. President Obama traveled extensively during his first year in office to help develop good relations with foreign governments.

GLOBAL TERRORISM

Throughout the 2000s, global terrorism has been on the rise. The United States doesn't always fight a single enemy army; it also fights a set of beliefs held by a group— such as al-Qaeda or ISIS—made up of terrorists in different locations. The 9/11 attacks in New York showed that people from these groups will die to support their beliefs. In the coming years, the challenge for future presidents will be to try to find peaceful solutions within and between cultures, to make the world safer for everyone.

JANUARY 17, 1991
Operation Desert Storm begins in Iraq (see page 71).

2001
9/11 attack and invasion of Afghanistan (see page 75).

MARCH 19, 2003
U.S. troops invade Iraq (see page 75).

MAY 2, 2011
Osama bin Laden found and killed by U.S. Navy SEALS (see page 77).

James Carter 1977-1981

James (Jimmy) Carter

Born in Plains, Georgia, James (Jimmy) Carter grew up on the family's peanut farm and later went to the U.S. Naval Academy. In 1970, he became Governor of Georgia, where he began campaigning on ecology and equality for African Americans. As President, Carter was also confronted with economic problems, an energy shortage, and several international conflicts.

FAST FACTS

39th President of the USA
Born: October 21, 1924
Term: 1977–1981 **Party:** Democratic
First Lady: Rosalynn Smith
Vice President: Walter F. Mondale

ENERGY CRISIS

During Carter's term, foreign oil prices became sky-high, and a nationwide energy shortage followed. Gas stations ran out of gas, which was rationed. Because the United States used so much oil, this energy crisis caused massive inflation (where money loses value and prices go up) and a recession. President Carter tried to reduce the use of foreign oil to help tackle the crisis.

▼ A long line of cars forms outside a gas station during the energy crisis of 1979.

President Carter mediated a peace treaty to help stop the 30-year conflict between Israel and Egypt. In September 1978, he met with Israeli Prime Minister Menachem Begin and Egyptian President Anwar Sadat to negotiate a resolution. The Camp David Accords was signed in 1979, and its success led later U.S. presidents to follow in Carter's footsteps to help solve international disputes.

▲ *The leaders of Egypt and Israel are cheered by Congress following the Camp David Accords.*

IRAN HOSTAGE CRISIS

In 1979, a group of Iranian students took over the U.S. Embassy in Iran, and 52 American diplomats and citizens were taken hostage. President Carter tried to negotiate a peaceful solution, but the hostages were kept for 444 days. The country blamed President Carter for not doing enough, even though the hostages were set free on his last day as President.

CARTER CENTER

Since leaving the presidency, Jimmy Carter has continued to work for human rights, health, and world peace. In 1982, he and his wife, Rosaylnn Carter, founded the Carter Center, a charity dedicated to these aims. Jimmy Carter works as a freelance ambassador for international conflicts and advises presidents on Middle East problems. In 2002, he won the Nobel Peace Prize for decades of service in trying to solve world conflicts peacefully.

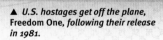

▲ *U.S. hostages get off the plane, Freedom One, following their release in 1981.*

Ronald Reagan 1981–1989

Ronald Reagan wasn't always a politician. Following a youth spent in Tampico, Illinois, he took up acting in the 1930s, becoming a minor Hollywood star. His political career began as Governor of California in 1966. From 1981, Reagan was a very popular President, working to raise the nation's prosperity and to gain "peace through strength" in foreign affairs.

FAST FACTS

40th President of the USA
Born: February 6, 1911
Died: June 5, 2004
Terms (two): 1981–1989
Party: Republican
First Lady: Nancy Davis
Vice President: George H. W. Bush

MILITARY MOVES

Wanting to make the U.S. military stronger, President Reagan gave 35 percent more money to defense. To deter international terrorism, in 1986, he ordered a bomb strike on Libya after American soldiers were attacked in a nightclub in West Berlin.

NUCLEAR WEAPONS TREATY

To try to end the Cold War, President Reagan negotiated a ban on the use of nuclear weapons with the Soviet leader, Mikhail Gorbachev. The 1987 Intermediate-Range Nuclear Forces treaty was followed by further agreements.

REAGAN REVOLUTION

President Reagan spearheaded a program—known as the "Reagan Revolution"—to help the economy grow and create wealth for Americans. He asked Congress to pass bills to stop inflation, cut taxes, and increase employment.

▲ Ronald Reagan and Mikhail Gorbachev hold discussions in 1985.

George H. W. Bush 1989–1993

A war hero who flew **58** missions for the U.S. Navy during World War II, George H. W. Bush's later political career included stints as a congressman and a U.N. ambassador. After serving as Ronald Reagan's Vice President, he became President himself, promising to use U.S. power as "a force for good."

FAST FACTS

41st President of the USA
Born: June 12, 1924
Term: 1989–1993 **Party:** Republican
First Lady: Barbara Pierce
Vice President: Dan Quayle

▼ *West Berlin citizens climb on top of the Berlin Wall in 1989.*

BERLIN WALL FALLS

Soviet leader Mikhail Gorbachev continued talks with U.S. Presidents Reagan and Bush, and by 1990–91, the Cold War between the United States and Soviet Union was over. The Berlin Wall—a symbol of Communism that divided East and West Berlin—was demolished as the world watched and cheered.

FIRST GULF WAR

When Iraqi dictator Saddam Hussein invaded Kuwait in 1991, President Bush sent in 425,000 U.S. troops to try to free the country. U.S. allied nations sent in 118,000 troops to help. Operation Desert Storm succeeded in defeating Iraq's army of a million troops in six months.

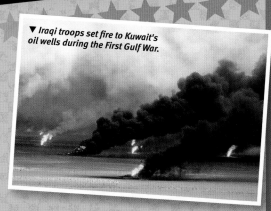

▼ *Iraqi troops set fire to Kuwait's oil wells during the First Gulf War.*

Bush was the first sitting Vice President to be elected President since 1836.

William J. Clinton
1993–2001

Born in Hope, Arkansas, William J. (Bill) Clinton studied at Georgetown and Oxford, later receiving a law degree from Yale. A meeting with President John Kennedy as a teenager inspired his political career. In 1979, he became Governor of Arkansas, working with his wife, Hillary. During his presidency, the U.S. economy boomed, although Clinton endured problems in his private life.

FAST FACTS

42nd President of the USA
Born: August 19, 1946
Terms (two): 1993– 2001
Party: Democratic
First Lady: Hillary Rodham
Vice President: Albert Gore, Jr.

THE HOME FRONT

Clinton started programs that increased the minimum wage and reduced crime rates, unemployment, and inflation. He balanced the U.S. budget so well that it had a surplus of money for the first time in decades. The President also tried to make stronger laws on the environment and gun sales.

FIRST LADY

In 1993, First Lady Hillary Clinton led the task force on National Health Care Reform. A lawyer and politician herself, she was Senator for New York in 2000 and U.S. Secretary of State from 2009 to 2013. In 2008, she was unsuccessful in her bid to be the Democratic presidential candidate.

▼ Hillary Clinton made a second bid for presidency, becoming a candidate in the 2016 elections.

Bill Clinton plays the saxophone and once wanted to be a professional musician.

President Clinton appointed more women to his Cabinet than any previous President. They included the first female Secretary of State, Madeleine Albright; the first female Attorney General, Janet Reno; and first female and first African-American Secretary of Energy, Hazel R. O'Leary.

▲ Madeleine Albright, who served as Secretary of State from 1997–2001.

▲ Hazel R. O'Leary, who served as the first female Secretary of Energy from 1993–1997.

INTERNATIONAL MISSIONS

In order to stop violence against civilians, President Clinton sent in U.S. peacekeeping forces to join NATO forces in Bosnia and Kosovo in 1995. That same year, he visited Northern Ireland, helping to end the conflict that had raged there for years.

OPERATION DESERT FOX

When dictator Saddam Hussein refused to allow United Nations' inspections of possible weapons of mass destruction, President Clinton ordered bombs to be dropped on Iraq. Operation Desert Fox lasted four days in December 1998 and targeted military and ammunition sites.

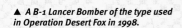

▲ A B-1 Lancer Bomber of the type used in Operation Desert Fox in 1998.

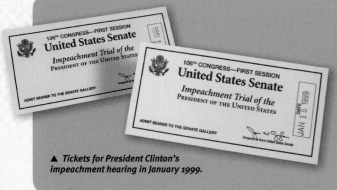

▲ Tickets for President Clinton's impeachment hearing in January 1999.

IMPEACHMENT

Due to circumstances around an affair with Monica Lewinsky, a young female intern at the White House, in 1998, Clinton was the second president in U.S. history to be **impeached**. The President was found not guilty of charges against him and continued serving his term.

George W. Bush 2001–2009

George W. Bush became the second U.S. President whose father had also been president. Early in his first term, in September, 2001, the United States suffered the most serious terrorist attack in its history. As a result, Bush spent much of his time in office waging war on international terrorism, as well as boosting education spending and cutting taxes.

FAST FACTS

43rd President of the USA
Born: July 6, 1946
Terms (two): 2001–2009
Party: Republican
First Lady: Laura Welch
Vice President: Richard B. Cheney

BUSH VS. GORE

The election between George W. Bush and Democratic candidate Vice President Al Gore in 2000 was so close that the Supreme Court made the final decision. Some people felt the Florida votes had been rigged and should have been recounted, but Bush was declared the overall winner by only five electoral votes.

EDUCATION BILL

Bush signed the No Child Left Behind Act of 2001 to reform education. It aimed to ensure a good education for those children most in need, who would be able to read by the end of third grade. The Act also gave money to pay for children to move from dangerous schools to safer ones.

In 2005, Hurricane Katrina destroyed parts of Louisiana, Mississippi, and Alabama.

Just months into Bush's presidency, an unprecedented crisis occurred. On September 11, 2001 (9/11), terrorists hijacked airplanes, crashing them into the World Trade Center in New York and the Pentagon in Washington. The flights were full of people and so were the buildings—almost 3,000 people died. America—and the whole world—reeled from the shock.

▶ *The remains of the World Trade Center after the 9/11 attacks.*

AFGHANISTAN INVASION

The terrorists responsible for 9/11 were an international group called al-Qaeda, led by Osama bin Laden. President Bush asked the Taliban—Islamic fundamentalists in Afghanistan—to hand him over, but they refused. So late in 2001, Bush sent U.S. troops to invade Afghanistan and find bin Laden.

▼ *U.S. troops move into position in the hills of Kowndalan, Afghanistan.*

INVADING IRAQ

In 2003, President Bush ordered the U.S. invasion of Iraq, claiming its leader, Saddam Hussein, was hiding weapons of mass destruction. U.S. forces quickly took control of the capital, Baghdad. Later, Hussein was captured and executed for crimes against humanity. Despite early successes for the United States, constant Iraqi opposition saw the war drag on.

▼ *U.S. tanks patrol the streets of the Iraq capital, Baghdad, in 2003.*

Barack Obama
2009–2017

Born in Hawaii, Barack Obama's mother was from Kansas and his father was from Kenya. He went to Columbia and Harvard Law School, and taught law at the University of Chicago before becoming an Illinois senator. In 2009, Barack Obama became the first African-American President of the United States, spending both his terms dealing with economic recovery, conflicts in the Middle East, and passing healthcare reforms.

FIRST LADY MICHELLE

A lawyer, writer, and mother to Malia and Sasha, Michelle Obama became the first African-American First Lady in 2009. She has worked with many community programs, including those designed to help young people and military families, tackle childhood obesity, and inspire children to higher education.

FAST FACTS

44th President of the USA
Born: August 4, 1961
Terms (two): 2009–2017 **Party:** Democratic
First Lady: Michelle Obama
Vice President: Joseph R. Biden, Jr.

▼ Standing alongside his wife, Barack Obama is sworn in as the 44th President of the United States in 2009.

A record 1.8 million people gathered to hear Obama's inaugural address in 2009.

BIN LADEN KILLED

Intelligence agencies had information that al-Qaeda leader Osama bin Laden was hiding near Abbottabad, Pakistan, so President Obama ordered an attack. On May 1, 2011, a team of U.S. Navy SEALS found and killed bin Laden.

▼ *Obama and his national security team watch a live feed of the military attack on Osama bin Laden.*

Ever since President Harry Truman, Democratic presidents have tried to pass healthcare reforms. In 2010, President Obama finally persuaded Congress to pass the Affordable Care Act. The Act aims to provide all Americans with affordable healthcare insurance, no matter what their income, age, or gender, so that they can receive medical care when they need it.

WAR IN IRAQ ENDS?

President Obama had been against the war with Iraq from its start. He promised to withdraw U.S. forces as soon as possible, and by 2011, the last U.S. troops left Iraq. However, the rise of Islamic extremists in the region saw U.S. forces return in 2014, along with personnel from other countries.

▲ *The last convoy of U.S. troops leaves Iraq in 2011.*

GLOSSARY

ABOLITIONIST
Someone who wants something banned—such as slavery.

BILL
A proposed law. When a bill has been passed by Congress, it becomes law.

BILL OF RIGHTS
A set of ten amendments to the U.S. Constitution designed to preserve the rights of states and individuals.

CABINET
The most senior members of the U.S. government. Cabinet members are nominated by the President and approved by Congress.

CIVIL RIGHTS
The rights of citizens to be treated equally under the law and to have the same opportunities as one another.

CIVIL WAR
A conflict between different factions, groups, or regions in the same country.

COLD WAR
A period of rivalry between the USA (and allies) and the Soviet Union (and allies) from the end of World War II to 1991.

COMMUNIST
Someone who believes there should be common ownership of a country's property and industries.

CONFEDERATE
Belonging to, or supporting, the Southern states, known as the Confederacy, during the U.S. Civil War.

CONGRESS
The legislative branch of the U.S. government made up of the Senate and the House of Representatives.

CONSTITUTION
The basic rules and principles by which a nation, such as the USA, is governed.

CONTINENTAL ARMY
The military forces of the 13 colonies that fought against British rule during the Revolutionary War.

CONTINENTAL CONGRESS
The governing body of the 13 colonies during the Revolutionary War.

CORRUPTION
Engaging in dishonest practices, often for financial gain.

DECLARATION OF INDEPENDENCE
The document that declared the USA to be a new nation, separate from Britain.

DESEGREGATED
To be equal and no longer kept apart—not treating social or racial groups in a society differently.

ECONOMIC DEPRESSION

A period of severe economic problems, usually resulting in businesses going bankrupt and very high unemployment.

ELECTORAL VOTE

A vote cast by an elector in U.S. presidential elections. It is these electors who directly vote for the President, based on the votes of the citizens.

FEDERAL

Applying to the whole country rather than just individual states.

FREE STATE

A state where people did not own slaves before the U.S. Civil War.

HOMESTEAD

Land granted by the government where people could live and grow their own food. The U.S. government encouraged homesteading as a way of populating rural parts of the country in the late 19th century.

IMPEACH

To charge an official with misconduct.

INAUGURATION

The official beginning of a U.S. President's term in office.

PARTY

A group of people with the same political aims.

RECONSTRUCTION

The rebuilding and reforming of the Southern states after the Civil War.

REPRESENTATIVE DEMOCRACY

A political system in which the people vote for officials to represent them in making decisions and passing laws.

SEGREGATION

Treating racial groups differently. Many Southern states had laws that kept black and white people apart and forced them to use separate facilities.

SECEDE

To withdraw from a union or alliance.

SLAVERY

Denying people their freedom and forcing them to work. Before the Civil War, many black people in the Southern states were forced to be slaves.

TARIFF

A tax charged on exports or imports.

UNION

A federation of states. In the Civil War, the country split into the Union in the North and the Confederacy in the South.

WHIG

A U.S. political party that was active between the 1830s and 1850s.

INDEX

Picture credits (t=top, b=bottom, l=left, r=right, c=center, fc=front cover, bc=back cover)

All images public domain unless otherwise indicated:
Dreamstime: bcb, 4bl Chris Minor, 4–5b John Bilous, 5tr Brandon Bourdages, 12–13b Americanspirit, 42–43b Mariusz Blach, 43cl Dani3315.
Wikimedia Commons: 10cr Daderot, 10br Bonnachoven, 32br Matthew Gordon, 66c Raphaël Thiémard, 71cl Sue Ream.